Theodore Roosevelt: The Progressive President

In the annals of American history, few figures stand as tall as Theodore Roosevelt. His legacy is one of boundless energy, rugged individualism, and unwavering dedication to public service. Born on October 27, 1858, in a brownstone house on East 20th Street in New York City, Theodore Roosevelt would grow up to become one of the most iconic and influential figures in the nation's history.

From a young age, Roosevelt displayed an insatiable curiosity and a deep connection to the natural world. He suffered from severe asthma, a condition that would plague him throughout his life, often forcing him to remain indoors. Despite his physical limitations, young Theodore developed a passion for nature and wildlife. He spent hours reading about animals and exploring the countless specimens he collected, creating his own "Roosevelt Museum of Natural History" in his home.

Theodore's early years were marked by family tragedy. His father, Theodore Roosevelt Sr., passed away in 1878, and six years later, in 1884, his mother, Martha "Mittie" Roosevelt, died of typhoid fever. These losses had a profound impact on young Theodore, shaping his character and instilling in him a sense of determination and resilience that would define his life's journey.

Roosevelt's love for the outdoors and a desire for

physical vigor led him to the Dakota Badlands in the 1880s, where he became a cattle rancher and a deputy sheriff. It was in the rugged, unforgiving terrain of the West that he honed the spirit of the cowboy. He became known as the "Rough Rider," a moniker that would follow him throughout his political career.

In 1886, Roosevelt married his childhood sweetheart, Alice Lee. However, their happiness was short-lived as Alice died of nephritis just two days after giving birth to their daughter, Alice. Stricken with grief, Theodore retreated to the Badlands but remained devoted to his daughter and his responsibilities.

Theodore Roosevelt's entrance into politics was marked by his appointment as a Civil Service Commissioner under President Benjamin Harrison. He made waves by actively working to combat corruption in the civil service, and his reformist zeal earned him recognition and respect. This was only the beginning of his political ascent.

Roosevelt's leadership qualities and determination came to the forefront during the Spanish-American War. He resigned from his position as Assistant Secretary of the Navy to lead the famous Rough Riders, a volunteer cavalry unit, in Cuba. His bravery during the Battle of San Juan Hill became legendary and catapulted him to national fame.

Following his notable leadership during the wars, Roosevelt returned to the United States and embarked on a new chapter of his political career. He was elected as the Governor of New York, a role in which he continued to champion progressive policies and reforms. Roosevelt's governorship was characterized by his strong support for the middle class, and he introduced innovative practices such as holding regular press conferences, a novelty at the time that allowed him to directly communicate with the public and the media. This approach earned him a reputation as an open and accessible leader.

Roosevelt's path took an unexpected turn when he assumed the role of Vice President of the United States after the untimely death of then-Vice President Garret Hobart. In this position, he had the opportunity to influence national policy and further prepare for a larger role in American politics. His experiences as Governor of New York and Vice President would play a pivotal role in shaping his later achievements as the 26th President of the United States.

The Presidential Years

In 1901, Theodore Roosevelt assumed the presidency, becoming the nation's 26th President, following the assassination of President William McKinley. At the age of 42, he was the youngest person to ever hold the office. His presidency marked a turning point in American history, as he ushered in a new era of progressivism and reform.

Roosevelt's domestic policies were marked by a commitment to curbing the power of monopolistic corporations. He earned the nickname "Trust-Buster" for his aggressive enforcement of antitrust laws and the breakup of major monopolies. He also championed conservation, setting aside vast swaths of public land as national parks, forests, and monuments, ensuring the preservation of America's natural beauty for future generations.

Roosevelt's vision for America was encapsulated in his Square Deal, a set of policies aimed at balancing the interests of labor, business, and the public. He advocated for workers' rights, consumer protection, and fair business practices. His efforts to mediate labor disputes, such as the Coal Strike of 1902, earned him a reputation as a champion of fairness and justice.

One of the most ambitious projects of Roosevelt's presidency was the construction of the Panama Canal. Under his leadership, the United States took control of the construction efforts and completed the canal, significantly reducing the time and cost of shipping between the Atlantic and Pacific Oceans.

Roosevelt's foreign policy was characterized by his belief in speaking softly and carrying a big stick. He mediated the end of the Russo-Japanese War, earning a Nobel Peace Prize for his efforts. His "Corollary" to the Monroe Doctrine asserted the United States' role in policing the Western Hemisphere, while his willingness to use military force, such as in the case of the "Great White Fleet," bolstered American influence abroad.

In the election of 1904, Roosevelt won a landslide victory, capitalizing on his popularity and accomplishments. His presidency had earned him the support of both the Republican Party and the Progressive movement, and he was elected to a full term.

Roosevelt chose not to seek re-election in 1908, and his handpicked successor, William Howard Taft, took office. However, he soon found himself at odds with Taft over the direction of the Republican Party. In 1912, Roosevelt ran for president as a Progressive Party candidate in one of the most memorable and competitive elections in American history.

Despite his third-party run, Roosevelt did not win the presidency in 1912, but his influence persisted. His progressive ideas left an indelible mark on American politics. He continued to be an advocate for social justice, conservation, and strong executive leadership until his death in 1919.

Theodore Roosevelt's presidency was a time of great reform and change in America. His energetic and dynamic leadership style, coupled with his unyielding dedication to progressive principles, transformed the nation. His commitment to justice and conservation, and his embodiment of the 'can-do' spirit continue to shape the nation's identity, making him one of the most beloved and influential figures in American history.

Major Policies of Theodore Roosevelt

Theodore Roosevelt, often referred to as "Teddy" or "TR," was a multifaceted and dynamic leader with a range of major ideas and philosophies that shaped his approach to politics and leadership. Here are some of the key ideas and philosophies associated with Theodore Roosevelt:

1. PROGRESSIVISM: Theodore Roosevelt was a staunch advocate of the Progressive movement, which sought to address the societal ills and inequalities brought about by the rapid industrialization of the late 19th and early 20th centuries. As President, he believed that government had a crucial role to play in mediating between big business and the working class. Under his leadership, progressive reforms included the regulation of railroads and trusts, labor protections, and consumer safeguards. For instance, the Meat Inspection Act and the Pure Food and Drug Act of 1906 aimed to ensure the safety and purity of food and drugs consumed by Americans, a response to the abuses and dangers in the food industry.

2. THE SQUARE DEAL: The "Square Deal" was Roosevelt's domestic policy platform, a testament to his dedication to fairness and equitable treatment for all Americans. This policy addressed the excesses of the Gilded Age, where monopolies and trusts wielded disproportionate power. By actively breaking up monopolies like Northern Securities and regulating big businesses, he aimed to level the playing field for smaller companies and prevent monopolistic

control. This approach was a significant step toward preventing corporate abuses and promoting economic fairness.

3. CONSERVATION: Roosevelt's love for nature and wildlife led to his profound commitment to conservation. He recognized the importance of preserving America's natural beauty for future generations. Under his presidency, he significantly expanded the national park system by creating the United States Forest Service and designating over 150 national forests, 51 federal bird reserves, and 18 national monuments. His actions ensured that America's breathtaking landscapes, such as the Grand Canyon and Yellowstone, remained protected and accessible to the public.

4. NATIONALISM: Theodore Roosevelt was a fervent nationalist, believing in America's unique role as a global power. His naval expansion, the construction of the Great White Fleet, was a symbol of American strength and deterrence. Moreover, his introduction of the "Roosevelt Corollary" to the Monroe Doctrine signaled America's commitment to preventing European intervention in the Western Hemisphere. This corollary asserted the United States' right to intervene in the internal affairs of Latin American countries if they were unable to meet their international financial obligations or maintain order. It asserted the United States as the dominant power in the Americas, reflecting Roosevelt's assertive approach to foreign policy and nationalism.

5. FOREIGN POLICY: Roosevelt's foreign policy mantra, "Speak softly and carry a big stick,"

encapsulated his approach to diplomacy. It meant negotiating from a position of strength while being open to peaceful resolutions. His mediation in the Russo-Japanese War and the Treaty of Portsmouth demonstrated his commitment to diplomacy and international peace.

6. ANTI-CORRUPTION AND TRUST-BUSTING: Theodore Roosevelt was a fervent advocate for combating corporate corruption and monopolistic practices. He believed that monopolies and trusts often undermined fair competition, exploited consumers, and stifled economic growth. Roosevelt took a proactive approach to break up and regulate these corporate giants. One of his most notable achievements in this regard was the antitrust case against Northern Securities Company, a railroad trust. He also brought successful antitrust cases against major corporations like Standard Oil and American Tobacco, demonstrating his commitment to preserving competition and preventing corporate abuse.

7. STEWARDSHIP OF THE PRESIDENCY: Roosevelt had a unique view of the presidency. He believed in the "bully pulpit," a term he used to describe the president's ability to use their position to influence and shape public opinion. He was an advocate for a strong executive branch and actively used his presidential powers to address pressing issues. One example of his stewardship of the presidency was his role in resolving the 1902 Coal Strike. He mediated between labor and management, ultimately securing better conditions for the workers and averted a nationwide energy crisis. This demonstrated his belief in the president's role as a mediator and problem solver.

8. MILITARY AND PREPAREDNESS: Roosevelt had a strong emphasis on military preparedness and modernization. He recognized that a strong military was crucial for national security and diplomacy. During his presidency, he initiated the construction of the Great White Fleet, a powerful naval force that circumnavigated the globe to demonstrate American naval strength. This move had a profound impact on American military prestige and deterrence.

9. INDIVIDUALISM AND SELF-IMPROVEMENT: Roosevelt was a strong proponent of individualism and personal responsibility. He believed in the importance of self-discipline, self-improvement, and the pursuit of one's best self. One example of this philosophy can be seen in his own life.
He overcame personal challenges, such as childhood illness and physical frailty, through his commitment to physical fitness, becoming an avid outdoorsman and a boxer. His personal resilience and commitment to self-improvement were reflected in his leadership style and values.

10. RACIAL EQUALITY: Roosevelt was an advocate for racial equality, although his actions were not always consistent with his rhetoric. He invited African American leader Booker T. Washington to the White House, signaling his support for civil rights and racial equality. However, due to the prevailing political climate of the time, he did not consistently push for civil rights legislation, reflecting the complexities of race relations during his era.

This book of Teddy Roosevelt provides further insight into his visionary thinking and principles, inviting readers to get to know the person behind the ideas even better.

The joy of living is
his who has the
heart to demand it.
Life is a great
adventure, and I
want to say to you,
accept it in such a
spirit.

We need intellect, and there is no reason why we should not have it together with character; but if we must choose between the two we choose character without a moment's hesitation.

No man can be a good citizen unless he has a wage more than sufficient to cover the bare cost of living, and hours of labor short enough so after his day's work is done he will have time and energy to bear his share in the management of the community, to help in carrying the general load.

Happiness lies not in the mere possession of money; it lies in the joy of achievement, in the thrill of creative effort. The joy and moral stimulation of work must no longer be forgotten in the mad chase of evanescent profits.

This country will not
be a permanently good
place for any of us to
live in unless we make
it a reasonably good
place for all of us
to live in.

I quote from the Progressive platform: "Behind the ostensible Government sits enthroned an invisible Government, owing no allegiance and acknowledging no responsibility to the people. To destroy this invisible Government, to dissolve the unholy alliance between corrupt business and corrupt politics is the first task of the statesmanship of the day..... This country belongs to the people. Its resources, its business, its laws, its institutions, should be utilized, maintained, or altered in whatever manner will best promote the general interest." This assertion is explicit. We say directly that "the people" are absolutely to control in any way they see fit, the "business" of the country.

We have no choice, we people of the United States, as to whether or not we shall play a great part in the world. That has been determined to us by fate, by the march of events. We have to play that part. All that we can decide is whether we shall play it well or ill.

It is the people, and not the judges, who are entitled to say what their constitution means, for the constitution is theirs, it belongs to them and not to their servants in office—any other theory is incompatible with the foundation principles of our government.

Patriotism means to stand by the country. It does not mean to stand by the president or any other public official, save exactly to the degree in which he himself stands by the country. It is patriotic to support him insofar as he efficiently serves the country. It is unpatriotic not to oppose him to the exact extent that by inefficiency or otherwise he fails in his duty to stand by the country. In either event, it is unpatriotic not to tell the truth, whether about the president or anyone else.

Criticism is necessary
and useful; it is often
indispensable; but it can
never take the place of
action, or be even a poor
substitute for it.
The function of the
mere critic is of very
subordinate usefulness.
It is the doer of deeds who
actually counts in the
battle for life, and not
the man who looks on and
says how the fight ought
to be fought, without
himself sharing the stress
and the danger.

Great thoughts
speak only to the
thoughtful mind,
but great actions
speak to all
mankind.

The only one who
makes no mistakes
is one who never
does anything.

It is essential
that there should be
organization of labor.
This is an era of
organization. Capital
organizes and therefore
labor must organize.

In the long run,
the most unpleasant
truth is a safer
companion than a
pleasant falsehood.

The farther one gets
into the wilderness,
the greater is the
attraction of its
lonely freedom.

Nothing in this world is worth
having or worth doing unless it
means effort, pain, difficulty.
No kind of life is worth leading
if it is always an easy life.
I know that your life is hard;
I know that your work is hard;
and hardest of all for those
of you who have the highest
trained consciences, and who
therefore feel always how much
you ought to do. I know your
work is hard, and that is why I
congratulate you with all my
heart. I have never in my life
envied a human being who led an
easy life; I have envied a great
many people who led difficult
lives and led them well.

No man is above the
law and no man is
below it; nor do we ask
any man's permission
when we require him
to obey it. Obedience
to the law is demanded
as a right; not asked
as a favor.

Many qualities are needed by a people which would preserve the power of self- government in fact as well as in name. Among these qualities are forethought, shrewdness, self-restraint, the courage which refuses to abandon one's own rights, and the disinterested and kindly good sense which enables one to do justice to the rights of others. Lack of strength and lack of courage and unfit men for self-government on the one hand; and on the other, brutal arrogance, envy — in short, any manifestation of the spirit of selfish disregard, whether of one's own duties or of the rights of others, are equally fatal.

The government is us;
We are the government,
you and I.

A great democracy has
got to be progressive
or it will soon cease
to be great or a
democracy.

In every civilized society property rights must be carefully safeguarded; ordinarily, and in the great majority of cases, human rights and property rights are fundamentally and in the long run identical; but when it clearly appears that there is a real conflict between them, human rights must have the upper hand, for property belongs to man and not man to property.

A vote is like a
rifle; its usefulness
depends upon the
character of the
user.

Freedom from effort
in the present merely
means that there has
been effort stored up
in the past.

When you are asked if
you can do a job, tell
'em, 'Certainly I can!'
Then get busy and
find out how to do it.

There is no room in this country for hyphenated Americanism...The one absolutely certain way of bringing this nation to ruin, of preventing all possibility of its continuing to be a nation at all, would be to permit it to become a tangle of squabbling nationalities.

Conservation is a great moral issue, for it involves the patriotic duty of insuring the safety and continuance of the nation.

The old parties are
husks, with no real
soul within either,
divided on artificial
lines, boss-ridden and
privilege-controlled,
each a jumble of
incongruous elements,
and neither daring to
speak out wisely and
fearlessly on what
should be said on the
vital issues of the day.

If, in any individual,
university training
produces a taste for
refined idleness, a
distaste for sustained
effort, a barren
intellectual arrogance,
or a sense of superfluous
aloofness from the world
of real men who do the
world's real work, then
it has harmed that
individual.

It is not often
that a man can make
opportunities for
himself. But he can
put himself in such
shape that when or if
the opportunities
come he is ready to
take advantage
of them.

In the great battle of
life, no brilliancy
of intellect, no
perfection of bodily
development, will count
when weighed in the
balance against the
assemblage of virtues,
active and passive, of
moral qualities which
we group together under
the name of character.

One of the fundamental necessities in a representative government such as ours is to make certain that the men to whom the people delegate their power shall serve the people by whom they are elected, and not the special interests. I believe that every national officer, elected or appointed, should be forbidden to perform any service or receive any compensation, directly or indirectly, from interstate corporations; and a similar provision could not fail to be useful within the States.

Women should have
free access to every
field of labor which
they care to enter,
and when their work
is as valuable as that
of a man it should be
paid as highly.

We wish to control big business so as to secure among other things good wages for the wage-workers and reasonable prices for the consumers. Wherever in any business the prosperity of the businessman is obtained by lowering the wages of his workmen and charging an excessive price to the consumers we wish to interfere and stop such practices. We will not submit to that kind of prosperity any more than we will submit to prosperity obtained by swindling investors or getting unfair advantages over business rivals.

The most successful
politician is he who
says what the people
are thinking most
often in the loudest
voice.

We stand equally against
government by a plutocracy
and government by a mob.
There is something to be
said for government by a
great aristocracy which has
furnished leaders to the
nation in peace and war for
generations; even a democrat
like myself must admit this.
But there is absolutely
nothing to be said for
government by a plutocracy,
for government by men very
powerful in certain lines
and gifted with "the money
touch," but with ideals
which in their essence are
merely those of so many
glorified pawnbrokers.

With a great moral
issue involved,
neutrality does not
serve righteousness;
for to be neutral
between right and
wrong is to serve
wrong.

A typical vice of
American politics —
the avoidance of saying
anything real on
real issues, and the
announcement of radical
policies with much sound
and fury, and at the same
time with a cautious
accompaniment of weasel
phrases each of which
sucks the meat out of the
preceding statement.

In any moment of
decision, the best
thing you can do is
the right thing, the
next best thing is the
wrong thing, and the
worst thing you can
do is nothing.

Nobody cares how
much you know,
until they know
how much you care.

Old age is like
everything else.
To make a success
of it, you've got to
start young.

The nation, like the individual,
cannot commit a crime with
impunity. If we are guilty of
lawlessness and brutal violence,
whether our guilt consists in
active participation therein or in
mere connivance and encouragement,
we shall assuredly suffer later on
because of what we have done. The
cornerstone of this republic, as of
all free governments, is respect for
and obedience to the law. Where we
permit the law to be defied or
evaded, whether by rich man or poor
man, by black man or white, we are by
just so much weakening the bonds of
our civilization and increasing the
chances of its overthrow, and of the
substitution therefore of a system
in which there shall be violent
alternations of anarchy
and tyranny.

The mother is the one supreme asset of national life; she is more important by far than the successful statesman, or business man, or artist, or scientist.

In a republic, to be successful we must learn to combine intensity of conviction with a broad tolerance of difference of conviction. Wide differences of opinion in matters of religious, political, and social belief must exist if conscience and intellect alike are not to be stunted, if there is to be room for healthy growth. Bitter internecine hatreds, based on such differences, are signs, not of earnestness of belief, but of that fanaticism which, whether religious or anti-religious, democratic or anti-democratic, is itself but a manifestation of the gloomy bigotry which has been the chief factor in the downfall of so many, many nations.

Here is your country. Cherish these natural wonders, cherish the natural resources, cherish the history and romance as a sacred heritage, for your children and your children's children. Do not let selfish men or greedy interests skin your country of its beauty, its riches or its romance.

No people is wholly
civilized where a
distinction is drawn
between stealing an
office and stealing a
purse.

It is no use to
preach to [children]
if you do not act
decently yourself.

Character, in the
long run, is the
decisive factor
in the life of an
individual and
of nations alike.

To discriminate against a
thoroughly upright citizen
because he belongs to some
particular church, or because,
like Abraham Lincoln, he has not
avowed his allegiance to any
church, is an outrage against that
liberty of conscience which is
one of the foundations of
American life. You are entitled to
know whether a man seeking your
suffrages is a man of clean and
upright life, honorable in all of
his dealings with his fellows, and
fit by qualification and purpose
to do well in the great office for
which he is a candidate; but you
are not entitled to know matters
which lie purely between himself
and his Maker.

The forces that tend
for evil are great and
terrible, but the forces
of truth and love and
courage and honesty
and generosity and
sympathy are also
stronger than
ever before.

I do not dislike but I certainly have no especial respect or admiration for and no trust in, the typical big moneyed men of my country. I do not regard them as furnishing sound opinion as respects either foreign or domestic business.

There are two things
that I want you to make
up your minds to: first,
that you are going to
have a good time as
long as you live - I
have no use for the
sour-faced man - and
next, that you are
going to do something
worthwhile, that you
are going to work hard
and do the things you
set out to do.

Far and away the best
prize that life has to
offer is the chance to
work hard at work
worth doing.

All forms
of success and
achievement lose
their importance
by comparison.

Any man who tries to
excite class hatred,
sectional hate, hate of
creeds, any kind of hatred
in our community, though
he may affect to do it in
the interest of the class
he is addressing, is in the
long run with absolute
certainly that class's
own worst enemy.

No man who is corrupt,
no man who condones
corruption in others,
can possibly do his
duty by the
community.

We admit with all sincerity
that our first duty is within
our own household; that we
must not merely talk, but act,
in favor of cleanliness and
decency and righteousness,
in all political, social, and
civic matters. No prosperity
and no glory can save a nation
that is rotten at heart.
We must ever keep the core of
our national being sound, and
see to it that not only our
citizens in private life, but,
above all, our statesmen in
public life, practice the old
commonplace virtues which
from time immemorial have
lain at the root of all true
national wellbeing.

Any political movement directed against any body of our fellow-citizens because of their religious creed is a grave offense against American principles and American institutions. It is a wicked thing either to support or oppose a man because of the creed he possesses. . . . Such a movement directly contravenes the spirit of the Constitution itself.

I believe that
the officers,
and, especially,
the directors, of
corporations should
be held personally
responsible when
any corporation
breaks the law.

If there is one tendency of
the day which more than any
other is unhealthy and
undesirable, it is the
tendency to deify mere
"smartness," unaccompanied
by a sense of moral
accountability. We shall
never make our republic what
it should be until as a people
we thoroughly understand and
put in practice the doctrine
that success is abhorrent if
attained by the sacrifice of
the fundamental principles of
morality.

I wish to preach, not the
doctrine of ignoble ease,
but the doctrine of the
strenuous life, the life of
toil and effort, of labor
and strife; to preach that
highest form of success
which comes, not to the man
who desires mere easy
peace, but to the man who
does not shrink from
danger, from hardship, or
from bitter toil, and who
out of these wins the
splendid ultimate
triumph.

The whole world is
bound together as never
before; the bonds are
sometimes those of
hatred rather than
love, but they are bonds
nevertheless. Frowning
or hopeful, every man
of leadership in any
line of thought or
effort must now look
beyond the limits of
his own country.

It is only through labor and painful effort, by grim energy and resolute courage, that we move on to better things.

Our government, National and
State, must be freed from the
sinister influence or control
of special interests. Exactly
as the special interests of
cotton and slavery threatened
our political integrity before
the Civil War, so now the great
special business interests too
often control and corrupt the
men and methods of government
for their own profit. We must
drive the special interests
out of politics.

Courage is not having
the strength to go on,
it is going on when
you don't have the
strength. Industry
and determination
can do anything that
genius and advantage
can do and many
things that they
cannot.

There can be nothing in the world more beautiful than the Yosemite, the groves of the giant sequoias and redwoods, the Canyon of the Colorado, the Canyon of the Yellowstone, the Three Tetons; and our people should see to it that they are preserved for their children and their children's children forever, with their majestic beauty all unmarred.

No man should receive a dollar unless that dollar has been fairly earned. Every dollar received should represent a dollar's worth of service rendered — not gambling in stocks, but service rendered. The really big fortune, the swollen fortune, by the mere fact of its size acquires qualities which differentiate it in kind as well as in degree from what is possessed by men of relatively small means. Therefore, I believe in a graduated income tax on big fortunes, and in another tax which is far more easily collected and far more effective — a graduated inheritance tax on big fortunes, properly safeguarded against evasion and increasing rapidly in amount with the size of the estate.

The things that will
destroy America are
prosperity-at-any-
price, peace-at-any-
price, safety-first
instead of duty-first,
the love of soft living,
and the get-rich-
quick theory of life.

To permit every lawless capitalist, every law-defying corporation, to take any action, no matter how iniquitous, in the effort to secure an improper profit and to build up privilege, would be ruinous to the Republic and would mark the abandonment of the effort to secure in the industrial world the spirit of democratic fair dealing.

Far better it is to dare
mighty things, to win
glorious triumphs,
even though checkered
by failure, than to take
rank with those poor
spirits who neither
enjoy much nor suffer
much, because they live
in the gray twilight
that knows neither
victory nor defeat.

Only those are fit to
live who do not fear
to die; and none are
fit to die who have
shrunk from the joy
of life and the duty
of life. Both life and
death are parts of the
same Great Adventure.

It is impossible to win the
great prizes of life without
running risks, and the
greatest of all prizes are
those connected with the
home. No father and mother
can hope to escape sorrow
and anxiety, and there are
dreadful moments when death
comes very near those we
love, even if for the time
being it passes by. But life
is a great adventure, and
the worst of all fears
is the fear of living.

There can be no effective control of corporations while their political activity remains. To put an end to it will be neither a short nor an easy task, but it can be done ... Corporate expenditures for political purposes, and especially such expenditures by public-service corporations, have supplied one of the principal sources of corruption in our political affairs.

It is not only highly desirable but necessary that there should be legislation which shall carefully shield the interests of wage-workers, and which shall discriminate in favor of the honest and humane employer by removing the disadvantage under which he stands when compared with unscrupulous competitors who have no conscience and will do right only under fear of punishment.

From the greatest
to the smallest,
happiness and
usefulness are
largely found in the
same soul, and the joy
of life is won in its
deepest and truest
sense only by those
who have not shirked
life's burdens.

The death-knell of the republic had rung as soon as the active power became lodged in the hands of those who sought, not to do justice to all citizens, rich and poor alike, but to stand for one special class and for its interests as opposed to the interests of others.

I care not what others think of what I do, but I care very much about what I think of what I do! That is character!

Right here let me make as vigorous a plea as I know how in favor of saying nothing that we do not mean, and of acting without hesitation up to whatever we say. A good many of you are probably acquainted with the old proverb: "Speak softly and carry a big stick—you will go far." If a man continually blusters, if he lacks civility, a big stick will not save him from trouble; and neither will speaking softly avail, if back of the softness there does not lie strength, power.

Get action. Do
things; be sane;
don't fritter away
your time; create,
act, take a place
wherever you are
and be somebody;
get action.

All contributions by
corporations to any
political committee
or for any political
purpose should be
forbidden by law.

It is a wicked thing to be
neutral between right and
wrong. Impartiality does
not mean neutrality.
Impartial justice consists
not in being neutral
between right and wrong,
but in finding out the
right and upholding it,
wherever found, against
the wrong.

We stand for a living wage. Wages are subnormal if they fail to provide a living for those who devote their time and energy to industrial occupations. The monetary equivalent of a living wage varies according to local conditions, but must include enough to secure the elements of a normal standard of living—a standard high enough to make morality possible, to provide for education and recreation, to care for immature members of the family, to maintain the family during periods of sickness, and to permit of reasonable saving for old age.

Knowing what's
right doesn't mean
much unless you do
what's right.

Order
without liberty
and liberty
without order
are equally
destructive.

We are passing through a period of great commercial prosperity, and such a period is as sure as adversity itself to bring mutterings of discontent. At a time when most men prosper somewhat some men always prosper greatly; and it is as true now as when the tower of Siloam fell upon all alike, that good fortune does not come solely to the just, nor bad fortune solely to the unjust. When the weather is good for crops it is also good for weeds.

The worst lesson
that can be taught
to a man is to rely
upon others and to
whine over his
sufferings.

People ask the
difference between
a leader and a boss.
The leader leads,
and the boss drives.

Where men are gathered together in great masses it inevitably results that they must work far more largely through combinations than where they live scattered and remote from one another... Under present-day conditions it is necessary to have corporations in the business world as it is to have organizations, unions, among wage workers.

Conservation means development
as much as it does protection.
I recognize the right and duty of
this generation to develop and use
the natural resources of our land;
but I do not recognize the right to
waste them, or to rob, by wasteful
use, the generations that come
after us. I ask nothing of the
nation except that it so behave
as each farmer here behaves with
reference to his own children.
That farmer is a poor creature
who skins the land and leaves it
worthless to his children. The
farmer is a good farmer who,
having enabled the land to
support himself and to provide
for the education of his children,
leaves it to them a little better
than he found it himself. I believe
the same thing of a nation.

The light has gone out of my life.

(diary entry, Feb. 14, 1884,
the day both his wife and
mother died within hours
of each other)

There is not a man of
us who does not at
times need a helping
hand to be stretched
out to him, and then
shame upon him who
will not stretch out
the helping hand
to his brother.

No man is worth
his salt who is not
ready at all times to
risk his well-being,
to risk his body, to
risk his life, in a
great cause.

Every man, who parrots the cry of 'stand by the President' without adding the proviso 'so far as he serves the Republic' takes an attitude as essentially unmanly as that of any Stuart royalist who championed the doctrine that the King could do no wrong. No self-respecting and intelligent free man could take such an attitude.

And those who oppose all reform will do well to remember that ruin in its worst form is inevitable if our National life brings us nothing whatever but a swollen and badly distributed material prosperity. In other words, I feel that material interests are chiefly good, not in themselves, but as an indispensable foundation upon which we should build a higher superstructure, a superstructure without which the foundation becomes worthless. Therefore I believe that the destinies of this country should be shaped primarily by moral forces, and by material forces only as they are subordinated to these moral forces.

While ever careful
to refrain from
wrongdoing others,
we must be no less
insistent that we are
not wronged ourselves.
We wish peace, but we
wish the peace of
justice, the peace of
righteousness. We wish
it because we think
it is right and not
because we are afraid.

Poverty is a bitter thing; but it is not as bitter as the existence of restless vacuity and physical, moral, and intellectual flabbiness, to which those doom themselves who elect to spend all their years in that vainest of all vain pursuits—the pursuit of mere pleasure as a sufficient end in itself.

Of one man in especial, beyond anyone else, the citizens of a republic should beware, and that is of the man who appeals to them to support him on the ground that he is hostile to other citizens of the republic, that he will secure for those who elect him, in one shape or another, profit at the expense of other citizens of the republic. It makes no difference whether he appeals to class hatred or class interest, to religious or anti-religious prejudice. The man who makes such an appeal should always be presumed to make it for the sake of furthering his own interest.

I am an American; free
born and free bred,
where I acknowledge
no man as my superior,
except for his own
worth, or as my
inferior, except for
his own demerit.

The lack of power to
take joy in outdoor
nature is as real a
misfortune as the
lack of power to
take joy in books.

It is not the critic who counts,
not the man who points out how
the strong man stumbled, or where
the doer of deeds could have done
better. The credit belongs to the
man who is actually in the arena;
whose face is marred by the dust
and sweat and blood; who strives
valiantly; who errs and comes
short again and again, because
there is no effort without error
or shortcoming; who knows the
great enthusiasms, the great
devotions and spends himself
in a worthy cause; who at the best,
knows in the end the triumph of
high achievement, and who, at
worst, if he fails, at least fails
while daring greatly; so that his
place shall never be with those
cold and timid souls who know
neither victory or defeat.

A soft, easy life is not worth living, if it impairs the fibre of brain and heart and muscle. We must dare to be great; and we must realize that greatness is the fruit of toil and sacrifice and high courage... For us is the life of action, of strenuous performance of duty; let us live in the harness, striving mightily; let us rather run the risk of wearing out than rusting out.

In the history of mankind
many republics have risen,
have flourished for a less or
greater time, and then have
fallen because their citizens
lost the power of governing
themselves and thereby of
governing their state; and in
no way has this loss of power
been so often and so clearly
shown as in the tendency to
turn the government into a
government primarily for the
benefit of one class instead
of a government for the
benefit of the people
as a whole.

No greater wrong can
ever be done than to
put a good man at the
mercy of a bad, while
telling him not to
defend himself or his
fellows; in no way can
the success of evil be
made surer or quicker.

Be practical as well
as generous in your
ideals. Keep your
eyes on the stars,
but remember to
keep your feet
on the ground.

With soul of flame and temper
of steel we must act as our
coolest judgment bids us.
We must exercise the largest
charity towards the wrong-
doer that is compatible with
relentless war against the
wrong-doing. We must be just
to others, generous to others,
and yet we must realize that
it is a shameful and a wicked
thing not to withstand
oppression with high heart
and ready hand. With
gentleness and tenderness
there must go dauntless
bravery and grim acceptance
of labor and hardship and
peril.

If you could kick the person in the pants responsible for most of your trouble, you wouldn't sit for a month.

The bosses of the
Democratic party and the
bosses of the Republican
party alike have a closer
grip than ever before on
the party machines in the
States and in the Nation.
This crooked control of
both the old parties by the
beneficiaries of political
and business privilege
renders it hopeless to
expect any far-reaching
and fundamental service
from either.

The good citizen will
demand liberty for himself,
and as a matter of pride he
will see to it that others
receive the liberty which
he thus claims as his own.
Probably the best test of
true love of liberty in any
country is the way in which
minorities are treated in
that country. Not only
should there be complete
liberty in matters of
religion and opinion, but
complete liberty for each
man to lead his life as he
desires, provided only that
in so doing he does not
wrong his neighbor.

www.ingramcontent.com/pod-product-compliance
Lightning Source LLC
Chambersburg PA
CBHW012259240726
48656CB00007B/2447